THINGS TO MAKE AND DO

All About Hanukkah

RABBI SHOSHANA BOYD GELFAND

ILLUSTRATED BY KATHRYN SELBERT

SCHOLASTIC

TO SCARLET, WHO LIGHTS UP THE WORLD JUST BY BEING IN IT — SBG
FOR MY FAMILY — KS

Published in the UK by Scholastic, 2022
1 London Bridge, London, SE1 9BA
Scholastic Ireland, 89E Lagan Road, Dublin Industrial Estate,
Glasnevin, Dublin, D11 HP5F

ISBN 978 07023 1584 8

A CIP catalogue record for this book is available from the British Library.

Printed by Bell & Bain Ltd., 303 Burnfield Road,
Thornliebank, Glasgow G46 7UQ
Paper made from wood grown in sustainable
forests and other controlled sources.

1 3 5 7 9 10 8 6 4 2

www.scholastic.co.uk

This copy of
All About Hanukkah:
Things to Make and Do
belongs to:

_____

_____

Learn all about the Hanukkah festival, celebrated every
year by 15.2 million Jewish people all over the world,
and the traditions associated with it!

This book is packed full of crafts and delicious recipes
for you to make and share with friends and family.

Don't forget: you can find definitions of the words
in **bold** in the glossary at the back of the book.

Judaism Around the World

Founded nearly 4,000 years ago in the Middle East, Judaism is the world's oldest **monotheistic** religious tradition.

Judaism is a religion and an ethnic category, which means some people are Jewish even if they don't believe in Judaism, while others can choose to become Jewish if they develop a belief in it!

Mizrahi Jews have Middle Eastern and North African ancestry, such as Iraq, Iran, Yemen and Morocco. **Sephardic Jews** are from Portugal and Spain. **Ashkenazi Jews** have German, French and Eastern European backgrounds. Judaism teaches certain beliefs and behaviours as below:

Beliefs

- that there is one God
- God gave Abraham (the first Jew) a covenant, a special agreement whereby God promises to look after the Jews and they promise to obey God's laws
- that the **Torah** is a holy book that contains God's teachings and advice as to how Jews should live
- the **Talmud** (collection of teachings from ancient **rabbis**) helps interpret the teachings in the Torah and how they can be applied to modern life

Behaviours

- from Friday evening until sunset on Saturday, Jews have a weekly day of rest, called **Shabbat**. This is a sacred time to share with God, family and your community
- visiting a synagogue (place of worship) during Shabbat and holidays
- many Jews follow rules about food, based on the Torah. These rules are called *kashrut*
- showing kindness and helping others, called **hesed** (or *chesed*)
- helping and repairing the world where possible (*tikkun olam*)
- giving **tzedakah** (charity)

 DID YOU KNOW?

There are more than 15 million Jews in the world, which is less than 0.2 per cent of the world's total population.

Israel is the only country in the world where the majority of the population are Jews – nearly 80 per cent of its citizens are Jewish.

Other countries with large Jewish populations include: USA, UK, France, Canada, Argentina, Germany, Russia, Australia, Brazil, South Africa, Ukraine, Hungary, Mexico and the Netherlands.

What is Hanukkah?

Many cultures have winter festivals that focus on lights. In ancient times, as the days started to get shorter and the weather got colder, winter celebrations helped people come together and keep each other hopeful that winter would end soon and the light of spring would arrive once again.

Hanukkah is a Jewish festival of lights. Hanukkah is based on a historical event that happened more than 2,000 years ago, when a Syrian king tried to stop Jews from worshipping their own God. Hanukkah is also based on a legend of a miracle when the lights almost went out. You'll have to decide for yourself whether you believe if that bit actually happened!

DID YOU KNOW?

For centuries parts of Europe, the Middle East, Africa and Asia had been ruled by various Hellenistic (ancient Greek-influenced) empires, including the Syrian Empire. Although the rulers were often not actually Greek, they brought Greek culture, language and religions to many ancient societies, including the Jews who lived in the Kingdom of Judea.

When is Hanukkah?

Most people now use the **Gregorian calendar**. It is a solar calendar, which means it uses the Sun to keep track of the changing seasons. But Judaism has its own calendar, which is thousands of years old. In the Jewish calendar we're not in the twenty-first century, we are now in the fifty-eighth century!

The Jewish calendar also has twelve months but it is a lunisolar calendar, and is based on the lunar (Moon) and solar (Sun) cycles. A new Moon is the start of a new month, and each month lasts until the next new Moon, which is twenty-nine or thirty days later.

Earth takes 365 days to travel around the Sun, but the Jewish calendar has 354 days in a year. To stay in sync with the Gregorian calendar, and to ensure that the Jewish festivals stay in the proper season, extra months are added to the Jewish calendar every two or three years. So even though Hanukkah is always on the twenty-fifth day of the Jewish month of *Kislev*, it isn't always the same date in the Gregorian calendar.

DID YOU KNOW?

Jewish days start and end at sunset. So if the first day of Hanukkah falls on 12 December in a particular year, the holiday actually begins at sunset on 11 December.

JEWISH CALENDAR

NISAN — נִיסָן
Pesach
Yom Hashoah

IYAR — אִייָר
Yom Ha'atzmaut
Lag Ba'omer

ADAR — אֲדָר
Purim

SIVAN — סִיוָן
Shavuot

SHEVAT — שְׁבָט
Tu Bishevat

TAMUZ — תַּמּוּז

TEVET — טֵבֵת

AV — אָב
Tishah Be-av

KISLEV — כִּסְלֵו
Hanukkah

ELUL — אֱלוּל

CHESHVAN — חֶשְׁוָן

TISHRI — תִּשְׁרִי
Rosh Hashana
Yom kipper
Sukot
Simchat Torah

JAN–FEB
FEB–MAR
MAR–APR
APR–MAY
MAY–JUNE
JUNE–JULY
JULY–AUG
AUG–SEPT
SEPT–OCT
OCT–NOV
NOV–DEC
DEC–JAN

SUN

| NEW MOON | WAXING CRESCENT | FIRST QUARTER | WAXING GIBBOUS | FULL MOON | WANING GIBBOUS | LAST QUARTER | WANING CRESCENT | NEW MOON |

Ancient Greece

Ancient Greece was not a united country, people lived in various city-states. In 359 BCE the kingdom of Macedonia, north of Greece, began to expand their territory and formed an **empire**. King Philip II conquered all the city-states, and in 334 BCE his son Alexander the Great expanded the empire and conquered land from Egypt to India. They spread Greek culture wherever they went, including their temples and gods. When Alexander died in 323 BCE, other leaders continued to spread Hellenistic (Greek-like) culture until the Romans took over, from 146 BCE.

There were twelve main gods who each had their own power over particular areas: Zeus (sky), Hera (women), Ares (war), Poseidon (sea), Demeter (harvest), Athena (wisdom), Apollo (Sun), Artemis (hunting), Hephaestus (fire), Aphrodite (love), Hermes (messenger) and Dionysius (wine). The Greeks built temples and statues to honour these gods and offered sacrifices to gain the gods' favour. However, Jews believe that there is only one God, and that statues or objects that represent God shouldn't be worshipped. The difference in religious practices led to conflict between the Jews and the Greeks.

In 175 BCE a Syrian ruler, Antiochus IV took over the Seleucid Empire, which had control of Israel. He was keen to spread Greek culture wherever he could. Antiochus believed that the Greek gods were on his side – and even that he was a god! – so he called himself Antiochus Epiphanes, which means "God Manifest" in Greek. Some of Antiochus's wittier enemies called him Antiochus Epimames instead, meaning "Antiochus the Madman". He built Greek cities in the countries he conquered, including several named after him, such as Epiphania in Armenia.

Fortress of Acra

DID YOU KNOW?

In about 168 BCE Antiochus IV had the Fortress of Acra built in Jerusalem. It was mentioned in the Book of Maccabees in the **Apocrypha**, but the fortress had been lost to time until its rediscovery in 2015.

Antiochus the King

Previous non-Jewish rulers let the Jews in Jerusalem, Israel, have their own Temple, as shown opposite, and pray to their God. Some Jews even adopted some Hellenistic customs, while others just continued as they'd always done.

But when Antiochus came to power he decided that everyone needed to be like him and he banned Jews from practising their religion. To make sure the Jews followed his rules, Antiochus robbed the Temple of its sacred objects, such as a seven-branched **menorah** (gold candelabra) that was always kept burning.

Antiochus didn't stop there and decided to put up a statue of the Greek god, Zeus, in the Jewish Temple. The statue went against the Jewish belief not to worship idols. Then Antiochus did the unthinkable; he sacrificed a pig on the altar. This was a deliberate insult to the Jewish religion as pigs are considered unclean under the rules of *kashrut*.

DID YOU KNOW?

Jews aren't allowed to eat certain foods, such as pork and shellfish, this is called *trefeh*. Jews are allowed to eat food, such as chicken or beef, if it is **kosher**. Jews who keep *kosher* also don't mix meat and dairy foods, but can eat neutral foods, such as vegetables, pasta and rice with both meat and dairy – these foods are called *parev*.

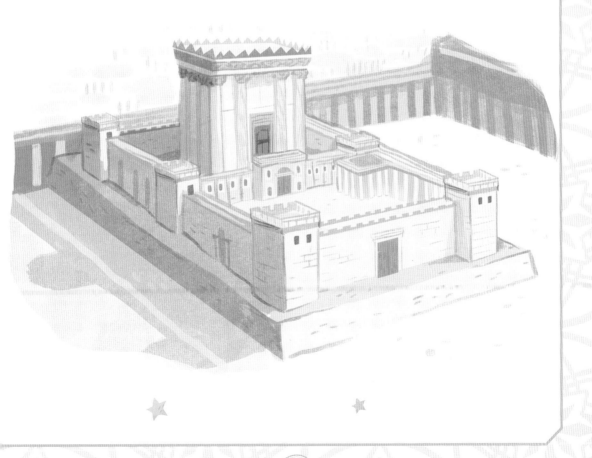

The Maccabees

In Modi'in, a town near Jerusalem, there lived a Jewish priest named Mattathias. One day, Greek soldiers demanded that he sacrifice a pig on the Temple's altar. Instead of following the soldiers' orders, he cried out, "Whoever is for God, follow me!"

He and his five sons – Jonathan, Simon, Judah, Eleazar and Yohanan – ran for their lives into the wilderness to hide in the caves there. Other Jews followed them, armed with the only weapons they had: spears, bows and arrows and rocks from their farms. The middle son, Judah, was a strong leader. He was given the title "Maccabee" in recognition of his leadership, and he and his brothers became known as the "Maccabees."

Judah knew he needed to defend his people, but how could a small group of villagers defeat a huge army?

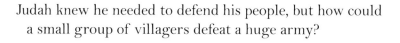

DID YOU KNOW?

Maccabee means "hammer" in Hebrew, and may have become Judah's nickname because he would strike against Antiochus's army with strength and speed.

The Few Against the Many

Judah knew that he couldn't win a war against the entire Greek army using force. There were just too many of them. So he had to be clever and make a few compromises. For example, at the beginning, the Jews refused to fight on Saturdays, which is the Jewish *Shabbat*, a sacred day of rest. But after many Jews were killed because of this, the Maccabees agreed that they would defend themselves, even on their holy day of rest.

The Maccabees fought for three years, defeating four armies, one after the other. Finally, they recaptured Jerusalem where their Temple stood and gained their independence. What happens next is what makes the famous story of Hanukkah.

DID YOU KNOW?

According to the Hebrew Bible, after six days, God completed the work of creation and decreed the seventh day, called *Shabbat*, to be a holy day of rest. Jews observe *Shabbat* as a day of rest when no work is done. Some Jews don't use electricity or go in a car on *Shabbat*. Others aren't so strict but will switch off phones and computers and spend time with family and friends.

Taking Back the Temple

The Maccabees got to work restoring the Temple. Judah and his men **reconsecrated** the Temple, removed the idols and built a new altar. Three years to the day after Antiochus took the temple – on the twenty-fifth day of the Jewish month of *Kislev* – the Maccabees had a dedication (Hanukkah) ceremony to celebrate. They offered a sacrifice to God on the new altar, lit the golden menorah (candelabra) and celebrated for eight days, giving thanks to God.

The celebration was similar to the eight-day dedication ceremony that King Solomon led when he built the first Temple hundreds of years earlier. The ceremony also borrowed elements from another Jewish holiday, *Sukkot* (a Jewish harvest festival) which is usually celebrated in September or October. *Sukkot* is a major Jewish festival, lasting eight days, which the Jews had loved celebrating in the Temple. As they had missed doing this for the past three years, they held a special *Sukkot*-like ceremony, waving palm branches and singing songs of praise to God as Jews do on *Sukkot*.

The Jews decided that every year, starting on the twenty-fifth of *Kislev*, Jews should celebrate for eight days to remember the miracle of them regaining the Temple and being able to worship freely as Jews.

The Miracle of the Oil

Everything you've read in the story up until now is based on historical records written close to the time that the events took place. But there is an additional part of the Hanukkah story, the legend of the oil, which only appears hundreds of years later in a sacred Jewish text called the Talmud.

The Talmud tells the Maccabees' story not as a military victory, but as a miracle, focusing on what happened when the Jews lit the menorah in the Temple.

In ancient times, they didn't use candles like we do today. They used a pot of olive oil with a string sticking out of it. As the string burned, it used up the oil. So in order to relight the menorah in the Temple, the Maccabees needed to find some olive oil. But the Greeks had destroyed it all, except for one small jar – enough to last just one day. It would take another week to make more pure oil. The Maccabees weren't sure what to do. Should they wait to light the menorah until they were sure they had enough oil to keep it going?

They decided to go ahead and light the menorah, expecting it to go out after twenty-four hours. But then a miracle happened. Instead of the oil lasting only one day, the menorah continued to burn for eight days. The rabbis in the Talmud give this as the reason that we celebrate Hanukkah for eight days – because it was a miracle that the oil lasted that long.

DID YOU KNOW?

The menorah in the temple has seven branches, but on Hanukkah, we light a menorah that has nine branches, one branch for each day of the miracle and an extra branch for the **shammash** – the helper candle that lights the other branches.

Where Are the Women?

The traditional story of Hanukkah focuses mostly on the men. That is because many of the people who wrote the history were men. But, there was a woman named Judith, who at the time was so exceptional that they wrote about her, too. Although her book is a part of the Apocrypha, it has has been excluded from the Hebrew Bible and only appears in the *Septuagint* (Greek version of the Hebrew Bible) – she even appears on a special menorah, as shown here.

However, Judith's story is probably fictional, and may have been written by a Jew during the Maccabean revolt to inspire the Jews to defend themselves against the enemy.

Judith's story is set hundreds of years before the Maccabees lived, but it has many similarities with their story, and has become so connected with the story of Hanukkah that we celebrate Judith during Hanukkah, too.

Judith was a young widow who lived in a town called Bethulia, near Jerusalem. When the Assyrian (modern-day Iraq as well as parts of Iran, Kuwait, Syria and Turkey) army invaded Israel, the Assyrian General Holofernes set out to conquer the Jews and stop them from practising their religion.

The Jews were terrified – the Assyrian army was huge! The people in Bethulia saw no option other than to surrender. But Judith persuaded them to wait to give her a chance to defeat the general.

Judith told Holofernes that he would be victorious, and so he asked Judith to have dinner with him. Holofernes's guards were sent away so they were alone. Judith fed him wine and cheese to make him sleepy. As Holofernes slept, Judith took his sword and cut off his head!

As the army was leaderless, the Jews were able to overcome them. And there was peace in the land due to the way Judith had saved her people.

DID YOU KNOW?

Judith (Yehudit in Hebrew) and Judah (Yehudah in Hebrew) are the masculine and feminine versions of the same name meaning "praise".

Hanukkah Customs

Light Candles

One of the most important rituals of Hanukkah is **Pirsum haNes** – talking about and sharing the miracle. Jews primarily do this by lighting Hanukkah lights and placing them in a window so that everyone can see them. In Israel and around the world, towns and cities hold public menorah lightings so everyone can share the ritual.

To hold the lights, we use a *Hanukkiah*, a special kind of menorah with space for eight candles (or oil lamps). In addition to the eight candles representing the eight days of the holiday, there is a shammash (helper) candle that is used to light the others.

DID YOU KNOW?

Hanukkiyot (Hanukkah menorahs) can vary in shape and size, but the eight candles should be the same height. However, the shammash can be placed higher or set off to the side, anywhere that sets it apart as special.

Eight Candles

In ancient times, only a single oil lamp was lit each of the eight nights of Hanukkah. In most homes, people could only afford to light a single lamp each night. However, some people liked to light one lamp on the first night and add a lamp each night, until there were eight lamps on the final night. This began the tradition of adding a candle on each night of Hanukkah.

When lighting the candles for Hanukkah there is a specific order in which they must be lit. Hanukkah lasts for eight nights, and on the

first night only two lit candles are placed in the *hanukkiah* (Hanukkah menorah): the shammash (helper) candle that has its own place on the menorah along with another candle that the shammash candle helped light. Every night, another candle is added. On the eighth night of Hanukkah, there will be nine lit candles, shining brightly.

As the Jews light the candles, they sing blessings giving thanks for the holiday of Hanukkah and the miracle of the oil lasting eight days.

DID YOU KNOW?

As Hanukkah lasts for eight days, it usually overlaps with *Shabbat*. However, lighting a fire during *Shabbat* is forbidden, so Jews make some adjustments by lighting the menorah on Friday evening while it is still light before *Shabbat* officially starts. On Saturday night, Jews wait until *Shabbat* has ended and light the next candle in the menorah once the sun has set.

★ Eat Foods Made with Oil ★

Because of the miracle of the oil, the foods we eat on Hanukkah tend to be fried in oil. But Jews fry different foods, depending on where they live in the world. In Israel, Jews cook *sufganiyot* (doughnuts), in eastern Europe they make *latkes* (potato pancakes), in Spain and South America, Sephardic Jews cook *buñuelos* (fried dough), Syrian Jews make *keftes de prasa* (vegetable fritters) and in India they make *gulab jamun* (fried milk solids). Although many of these recipes originated in specific parts of the world, they are now eaten everywhere and enjoyed year-round.

In addition to oily foods, Jews also eat cheesy foods on Hanukkah in memory of Judith who supposedly fed the general salty cheese to make him drink more wine. Some people just add cheese to their potato pancakes so they get both the oil and the cheese in one dish!

DID YOU KNOW?

In January 2021, the olive tree was voted as Israel's national tree. As well as providing a source of food which is also turned into olive oil, olives are an important symbol for Jews. In the Jewish Bible, in the story of Noah and the flood, when Noah released a dove to find out if there was land nearby the dove returned with an olive branch in its mouth. Because of this, doves and olive branches became a symbol of peace and continue to be so to this day.

Playing Games

As the Hanukkah candles burn, it is customary to sing songs and play games. A favourite Hanukkah game is called *dreidl* (the **Yiddish** word for a four-sided spinning top).

There are many stories about why *dreidl* is played on Hanukkah. One legend says that the ancient Jews used it to fool the Greeks who were **oppressing** them. Even though it was forbidden, the Jews continued to pray in secret. If a Greek soldier walked by while they were praying, they would just take out their *dreidl* and start to play that instead.

The *dreidl* letters have an extra meaning to spell out the message of Hanukkah:

> The letter *Gimel (Gadol)* – Great | The letter *Nun (Nes)* – Miracle
> The letter *Hay (Haya)* – Happened | The letter *Shin (Sham)* – There
> "(A) Great Miracle Happened There"

DID YOU KNOW?

In Israel, instead of the four letters spelling out "(A) Great Miracle Happened There", Israeli *dreidls* have a different fourth letter so it spells out "(A) Great Miracle Happened HERE"

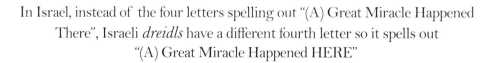

Giving Gelt

Money and chocolates are given as gifts on Hanukkah. A traditional gift on Hanukkah is *gelt*, which is a Yiddish word that means "money". Or you can give chocolate coins, which are not only fun to play with in *dreidl* but are also delicious to eat!

Some families also exchange small gifts with each other each evening, and also give to those who are needy so that they can celebrate the holiday, too.

DID YOU KNOW?

It is thought that coins became a common gift on Hanukkah as they were a way to remember that the Maccabees minted (made) their own coins when they defeated the Greek army.

Israel's Torch Relay

In modern-day Israel, there is an annual Hanukkah torch relay. It starts in the town of Modi'in, the home of Judah Maccabee and his family. Runners carry the torch to Jerusalem to celebrate Hanukkah, this marks the beginning of Hanukkah celebrations in Israel.

During the torch relay, people line the road from Modi'in to the Western Wall in Jerusalem's Old City. They pass the Hanukkah torch onwards, from person to person, until it reaches the Western Wall where the torch lights a giant *hanukkiah* (Hanukkah menorah) at the Western Wall.

DID YOU KNOW?

Taking place every four years, the international Jewish sports festival is called the "Maccabiah" in honour of the Maccabee family. The festival started in 1932, and is now almost as big an event as the Olympics. About 10,000 athletes attend each Games, from eighty countries, and compete in forty sports. The event is open to Jewish athletes from around the world, as well as Israeli athletes of any ethnicity or religion.

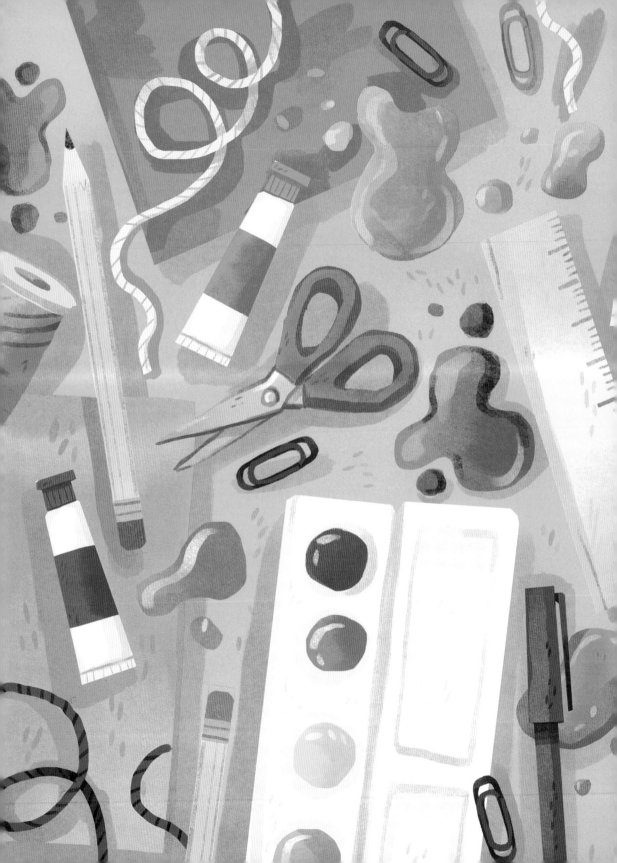

Art
&
Crafts

Make a Hanukkah Menorah

Let your imagination run wild when decorating this menorah.

You will need:

- 1 kitchen towel roll tube
- 8 toilet roll tubes
- scissors
- paint
- paintbrush
- liquid glue
- yellow, red or orange tissue paper

SAFETY FIRST
Ask an adult for help when using scissors.

Instructions:

1. Carefully cut the kitchen roll so that it is only a little bit taller than the toilet rolls. This is the shammash candle.

2. Paint and decorate the rolls and let them dry.

3. Line the rolls up and carefully glue them together.

4. To make the candles' flames, rip the tissue paper in half. Fold it in half and then fold it again.

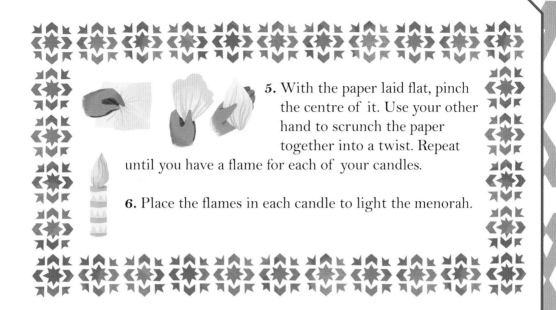

5. With the paper laid flat, pinch the centre of it. Use your other hand to scrunch the paper together into a twist. Repeat until you have a flame for each of your candles.

6. Place the flames in each candle to light the menorah.

TOP TIP:

The shammash doesn't need to be in the centre, it just needs to be different from the other eight candles. So feel free to be creative and put it at the end of the row or anywhere that sets it apart.

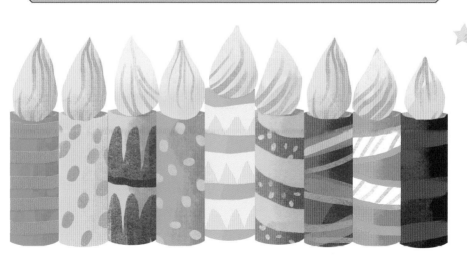

Make Dreidl Ornaments

Make this fun papercraft activity to add some colour to your home.

You will need:

- ruler
- several sheets of coloured paper
- scissors
- paint
- paintbrushes
- colouring pencils
- hole punch
- ribbon
- stapler

Instructions:

1. Use a ruler to measure out five strips of paper. You will need two 15 cm, two 10 cm and one 5 cm long strips of paper. They should all be 2 cm wide.

2. Use paint or colouring pencils to decorate your strips.

3. Arrange the mid-length strips in a half-circle around the short strip of paper, with the longer strips on the outside. Staple the strips together at the top and bottom.

4. Use a holepuncher to make a hole at the top of the ornament. Thread a ribbon through and hang it up. Make as many *dreidls* as you like.

SAFETY FIRST
Ask an adult for help when using scissors.

Make a Dreidl

Make your own *dreidl* and play it at home.

You will need:

- piece of tracing paper (or baking paper)
- pen
- piece of thick card or thin cardboard (such as a used cereal box)
- coloured felt-tip pens
- scissors
- tape
- pencil

SAFETY FIRST
Ask an adult for help when using scissors.

Instructions:

1. Trace the outline of the template on the opposite page onto tracing paper. Make sure to include the dotted lines!

2. Turn the tracing paper over and place it on your card. Draw over the lines you traced, pressing down heavily so that the drawing transfers onto your card.

3. Copy the Hebrew letters from the template onto your piece of card and decorate it now, if you want to.

4. Carefully cut around the template. Don't cut the dotted lines. Fold the dotted lines. Press hard to make strong folds.

5. Tape the card together. Leave a small hole at the top.

6. Push a pencil point through the top of the *dreidl* to make a handle. Turn the page to find out how to play!

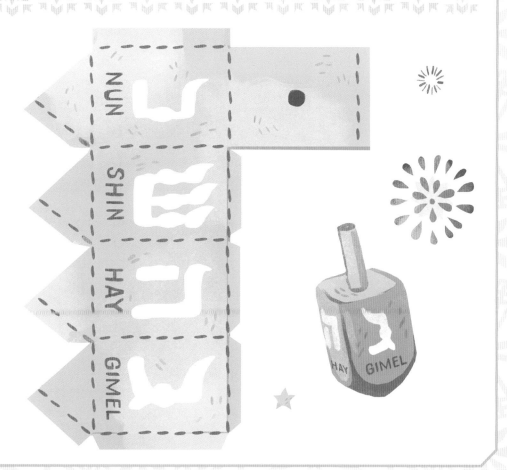

Learn to Play Dreidl

Now that you have your *dreidl*, you are ready to learn to play the game.

You will need:

- pile of small objects such as stickers, coins, wrapped sweets or Hanukkah *gelt* (gold chocolate coins)
- a *dreidl*

Instructions:

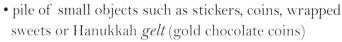

1. Each player starts with the same number of objects in a pile in front of them, such as ten objects each.

2. Before each turn, everyone puts one piece in the "pot" in the middle.

3. Each player takes a turn to spin the dreidl. Depending on what it lands on, that player has to do one of the following:

   Nun (*nisht*) or "nothing" – player gets nothing
   Gimel (*gantz*) or "everything" – player takes the entire pot
   Hay (*halb*) or "half" – player gets half of the pot
   (or round up if there is an odd number in the pot)
   Shin (*shtel*) or "put in" – player has to put a piece into the pot

4. Each player takes their turn to spin and does what the *dreidl* tells them to do.

5. When the pot is empty (or has only one piece left), each player must put one object into the pot.

6. If a player is out of pieces, they are out.

7. When one person has all of the pieces, they win (but they usually share the objects with everyone else, especially if they are chocolate!)

Make a Menorah

In the past before there was electricity, people used oil lamps to light their homes. Now we can use electric versions of our menorah candles, with battery-operated tea lights. Here is a menorah activity that you can make.

You will need:

- egg cartons
- scissors
- thin cardboard (such as a cereal box)
- paint
- paintbrush
- liquid glue
- battery-operated tea lights

SAFETY FIRST
Ask an adult for help when using scissors.

Instructions:

1. Cut up the egg carton to make ten cups and cut out a base from your cardboard.

2. Paint the cups and your base and leave to dry.

3. Glue the cups on to your base. To make the shammash (helper) candle higher, glue 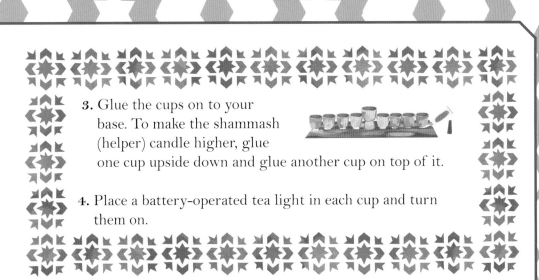 one cup upside down and glue another cup on top of it.

4. Place a battery-operated tea light in each cup and turn them on.

Make Wrapping Paper

Create fun wrapping paper for Hanukkah and other festivals.

You will need:

- medium-sized potatoes
- sharp knife
- acrylic paint
- paintbrushes
- roll of solid coloured paper

SAFETY FIRST
Ask an adult for help when using a knife.

Instructions:

1. Ask an adult to cut your potato in half so that you have two circles. Each potato half will make two stamps.

2. Ask an adult to carefully carve a triangle onto one potato. Carve another triangle of the same size on top of the other triangle, but the other way up. This is the Star of David, a six-pointed star.

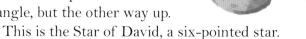

3. Ask an adult to carve off any potato bits outside of the star. This is your stamp.

4. On the other potato, draw a tall rectangle with a teardrop-shape on top of it. This is your candle. Ask an adult to carve out the shape.

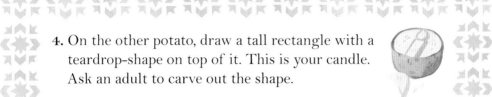

5. Now that your stamps are made, paint them any colour you want and start pressing them onto the paper to make a unique pattern!

TOP TIP:

Use different paintbrushes for each colour to stop the colours from running together. You can use other colours and designs.

Make Window Decorations

Hanukkah is all about telling people about the miracle, so window decorations are a great way to do that. Hang your decorations in a window to share the joy of Hanukkah with anyone who walks past.

You will need:

- lightweight craft paper
- ruler
- scissors
- coloured pencils
- felt-tip pens (optional)
- tape

SAFETY FIRST

Ask an adult for help when using scissors.

Instructions:

1. Cut a strip of paper around 10 cm wide and 25 cm long.

2. Fold the paper like an accordion: fold each strip back and forth on top of one another.

3. Draw a half a *dreidl* on the folded piece of paper. Make sure that you only draw along the side of the paper with the folded edge.

4. Cut along the design you traced, making sure the cut goes through all the layers of the paper.

5. Unfold the strip to reveal a chain of *dreidls*.

6. Use a pen to draw the letters: *nun, gimel, hay* and *shin* onto each of the *dreidls*.

7. Hang the paper *dreidls* in the window using tape.

TOP TIP:

Try cutting out other shapes using the same method. Can you figure out how to make other shapes for other festivals?

Make a Greeting Card

Create a *dreidl* card that actually spins when you open it!

You will need:

- 1 piece of card in different colours
- pen
- scissors
- 1 piece of white sewing thread
- needle
- tape

SAFETY FIRST
Ask an adult for help when using scissors/needles.

Instructions:

1. Fold a piece of card in half. This will be the main part of your card.

2. Draw a large *dreidl* on the front of your card and carefully cut it out.

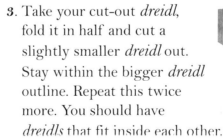
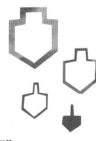

3. Take your cut-out *dreidl*, fold it in half and cut a slightly smaller *dreidl* out. Stay within the bigger *dreidl* outline. Repeat this twice more. You should have *dreidls* that fit inside each other.

4. You can now decorate the cut-outs. Lay the biggest cut-out down. Put the next biggest inside the cut-out. Ask an adult to use a needle and thread to sew through the top of the cut-outs.

5. Repeat step 4 with the rest of the cut-outs. Make sure to thread the string through the bottom of the cut-outs. Tape this to the inside of your card.

6. Once you stand the card up, the *dreidls* will spin around.

TOP TIP:

This technique will work with most shapes, so you can make cards for any occasion.

Recipes

SAFETY FIRST

Remember to ask an adult for help when using
any sharp equipment, such as knives, or attempting
a recipe that requires the use of an oven, hob
or electric blender. And have fun creating
and sharing these delicious treats!

Always ask an adult to help when cooking foods in oil.
Make these recipes with an adult and afterward you
and your family can have a Hanukkah feast.

Latkes (*Potato Pancakes*)

The common factor in most Hanukkah recipes is that they are fried in oil as this celebrates the miracle of the oil.

Always ask an adult to help when cooking foods in oil.

Ingredients

- 500 g potatoes
- 1 large onion
- 2 large eggs
- 2 tablespoons matzah meal (or unseasoned dry breadcrumbs)
- 1 teaspoon salt
- ground black pepper
- 1 teaspoon baking powder
- vegetable oil (for frying)
- apple sauce or sour cream (for topping)

Equipment

- box grater
- cheesecloth (or clean tea towel)
- large mixing bowl
- large frying pan
- ladle
- slotted spatula
- plate lined with paper towels

SAFETY FIRST

Ask an adult for help when using the hob, knife or grater.

Method

1. Peel an onion and cut the potatoes in half, but don't peel them. Ask an adult to grate the onion and the potatoes.

2. Put the grated mixture onto a clean cheesecloth. Gather the edges and squeeze out the liquid over a bowl.

3. Place the mixture into a large bowl. Add the eggs, matzah meal, salt, pepper and baking powder. Mix everything together and set it aside.

4. Ask an adult to pour some oil into the pan and put it on a medium heat. Ask an adult to drop a bit of the mixture into the pan – if it sizzles you can start cooking the *latkes*.

5. Ask an adult to carefully drop a ladleful of the latke mixture into the oil. Press it down with a spatula to make a pancake.

6. Repeat until the frying pan is full, making sure the *latkes* aren't touching. Cook each side for 4 to 5 minutes, until they are golden brown and crispy, then take them out and place on a plate lined with paper towels.

7. Serve with a dollop of apple sauce or sour cream on top of the *latkes*.

Sufganiyot (Doughnnuts)

In Israel, *sufganiyot* – jam-filled doughnuts – are a favourite Hanukkah treat. They are sold on the street and enjoyed all eight nights of Hanukkah.

> Always ask an adult to help when cooking foods in oil.

Ingredients

- 400 g plain flour, plus extra for kneading
- 7 g fast-action dried yeast
- 1 teaspoon salt
- 1 teaspoon caster sugar
- 2 tablespoons olive oil
- 200 ml water
- 1 litre vegetable oil (for frying)
- 200 g strawberry jam (for filling)
- 1 tablespoon icing sugar (optional)

SAFETY FIRST
Ask an adult for help when using the hob.

Equipment

- scales
- large mixing bowl
- wooden spoon
- cling film
- rolling pin
- tray lined with baking parchment
- medium pan
- slotted spatula
- chopping board
- round cookie cutter
- plate lined with paper towels
- skewer
- piping bag
- small sieve

Method

1. Mix all of the dry ingredients together in a bowl. Add the olive oil and the water. Mix it into a dough. If the dough is too rough, add a little water until it becomes smooth.

2. Sprinkle flour on a cutting board and place the dough onto it. Use your hands to knead the dough for 7 to 10 minutes until it is smooth.

3. Place the dough in a lightly oiled bowl and loosely cover it with cling film. Leave the dough to rise in a warm place for 1 hour.

4. Roll out the dough until it is 2½ cm thick. Use a cookie cutter to make lots of circles of dough and put them on a tray. Cover the tray with cling film. Set the dough aside for 30 minutes.

5. Pour vegetable oil into a saucepan – only fill half the pan. Heat the oil on a medium heat. Ask an adult to carefully place the doughnuts into the oil. Cook each side for 2 to 3 minutes.

6. Ask an adult to take the doughnuts out with a slotted spatula and place on a plate. Repeat with the rest of the doughnuts.

7. Ask an adult to use a skewer to poke a hole into the side of each doughnut. Fill a piping bag with jam and gently squeeze it into the doughnuts and serve.

TOP TIP:

You can fill your doughnut with anything you'd like – try other flavours of jam, or else caramel, chocolate or cream. Be creative!

Dreidl Appetisers

Ingredients

- 60 g hard cheese (havarti works well, but you can also try gouda)
- 4 thin pretzel sticks
- red pepper for garnish (optional)

Equipment

- knife
- skewer
- serving dish

SAFETY FIRST

Ask an adult for help when using a knife or skewer.

TOP TIP:

Try cutting the red pepper garnish in the shape of tiny Hebrew letters to decorate the face of the cheese *dreidl*.

Method

1. Cut the cheese into small cubes.

2. Ask an adult to use a knife to carefully cut the cubes so that the bottom of each cube ends in a point.

3. Use a skewer to poke a small hole into the top of the cheese cubes.

4. Cut each of the pretzel sticks into 3 cm pieces and stick each of them into the top of a cube to make the handle for each of your *dreidls*.

5. Garnish with red pepper before serving.

Menorah Waffles

Hanukkah celebrations usually happen in the evenings, as that's when candles are lit. But there's no reason not to celebrate all day long, you could give breakfast a fun Hanukkah twist with this tasty waffle recipe.

Ingredients

- 2 small rectangular waffles
- 1 clementine
- 9 raspberries
- decorations, such as chocolate chips, blueberries, raisins or nuts

Equipment

- knife
- plate

TOP TIP:

If you warm the waffles in the toaster first, then any chocolate chips that you decorate it with will get all gooey and delicious.

SAFETY FIRST

Ask an adult for help when using a knife.

Method

1. Carefully cut each waffle into a square shape, until you have two square waffles.

2. Place the two waffle squares next to each other to make the main part of the menorah.

3. Use the strips that you've cut off to make the stem and base of the menorah.

4. Decorate the menorah with chocolate chips, blueberries, raisins or nuts in the small squares. You can make whatever design you like with them.

5. Peel the clementine and separate the segments to make candles at the top of the menorah.

6. Add a raspberry to the top of each clementine slice to "light" the correct number of candles, depending on what day of Hanukkah it is – or how much you like raspberries!

Buñuelos (Fried Dough)

Sephardic Jews enjoy *buñuelos*, sometimes known as *bimuelos* on Hanukkah. This dessert is usually drizzled with honey or syrup.

> Always ask an adult to help when cooking foods in oil.

Ingredients

- 300 g plain flour
- 1 teaspoon baking powder
- a pinch of salt
- 1 large egg
- 250 ml whole milk
- 1 litre vegetable oil (for frying)
- honey (for topping)

Equipment

- scales
- large mixing bowl
- wooden spoon
- jug
- medium saucepan
- plate lined with paper towels
- slotted spatula
- teaspoon

SAFETY FIRST

Ask an adult for help when using the hob.

TOP TIP:

Sephardic Jews traditionally drizzle honey, but you can also use maple syrup or icing sugar.

Method

1. Mix the flour, baking powder and salt together in a large bowl.

2. Mix the egg and milk together and combine with the flour. Mix it all together.

3. Pour the vegetable oil into a saucepan – the oil should only fill half the pan. Ask an adult to heat the oil over a medium heat.

4. Ask an adult to use a teaspoon to carefully drop small amounts of batter into the oil. Fry each side of the *buñuelos* for 4 minutes. Once cooked, the *buñuelos* will be golden brown and feel light.

5. Ask an adult to use a slotted spoon to carefully lift the *buñuelos* from the oil. Place them on a plate to drain. Repeat with the remaining *buñuelos*.

6. Drizzle honey or icing sugar on top and serve immediately.

Edible Centrepiece

Ingredients

- ¼ cucumber
- 8 asparagus spears or long green beans
- 9 carrot sticks (one a bit longer than the others)
- 9 baby plum tomatoes cut in half

Equipment

- medium saucepan
- colander
- knife
- large serving platter

SAFETY FIRST

Ask an adult for help when using a knife.

TOP TIP:

Instead of vegetables, you could try making a centrepiece of fruit. Try using bananas for the menorah base and body, blueberries for the nine "arms" of the menorah, apple slices for the candles and orange slices for the flames.

Method

1. Fill a saucepan with water and bring to a boil. Add the asparagus or green beans and simmer for 5 minutes, until it is cooked. Drain and set aside.

2. Cut the cucumber into circular slices. Place five to six slices in a vertical line. At the base of the line, make a horizontal line with six cucumber slices. This is the base and stem of the menorah.

3. Using the asparagus spears or beans, build eight branches onto your menorah, with four on either side of the cucumber stem.

4. Place carrot stick "candles" on top of each branch, with an especially big one in the middle for the shammash candle.

5. "Light" your carrot candles by adding half a baby plum tomato to the top of each one.

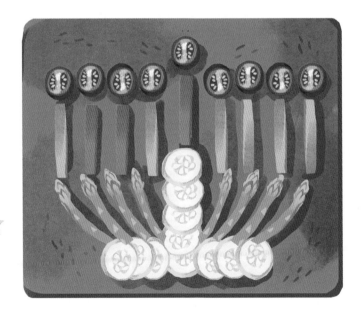

Hanukkah Challah

MAKING THE DOUGH
Ingredients

- 110 g margarine
- 350 ml warm water (or milk)
- 875 g plain flour
- 4½ teaspoons fast-action dry yeast
- 150 g granulated sugar
- 2 teaspoons salt
- 3 large eggs, whisked
- 2 egg yolks (to brush over the bread)
- few drops of vegetable oil

Equipment

- scales
- medium saucepan
- large mixing bowl
- chopping board
- clean tea towel (or cling film)
- knife
- large baking sheet lined with parchment paper
- small bowl for eggs
- pastry brush

Method

TOP TIP:
When you are kneading the dough, coat your hands with flour to keep them from getting sticky.

1. Mix the margarine and water over a medium heat until the margarine melts. Make sure it isn't too hot as that will deactivate the yeast in the next step.

2. In a bowl add 825 g of flour, the yeast, sugar and salt. Then add the margarine mixture and the eggs and mix everything together. Once it has all been combined, set it aside for 5 minutes.

3. Sprinkle flour onto a chopping board and place the dough onto it. Knead the dough for 10 minutes.

4. Add a bit of oil to a bowl and add the dough. Turn the dough to cover it in oil. Cover the dough with a tea towel and leave it to rise in a warm place for 2 hours.

5. Punch the dough down to its original size and set it aside for 10 minutes.

6. Separate the dough into six pieces, and shape five pieces into long coils. Lay one coil into a straight line, and bring the end together and carefully twist as per the picture.

7. Make four long coils, each one a bit shorter than the next. Lay the longest coil in a "U" shape on top of the twisted dough. Nest the next longest coil above the previous coil. Repeat with the remaining coils.

8. Cut the remaining dough into 9 small pieces. Shape them into balls and place on top of each "candle".

9. Cover the dough with a clean tea towel. Leave it to rise for 30 minutes in a warm place.

10. Preheat the oven to 180°C or gas mark 4. Whisk the egg yolks together and brush them on to the dough.

11. Cook for 25 to 30 minutes until the challah gets a golden brown colour.

SAFETY FIRST
Ask an adult for help when using the hob and oven.

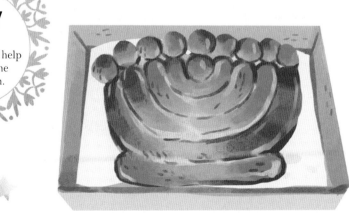

Gulab Jamun *(Sweet Dough Balls)*

Jews from India celebrate Hanukkah with a sweet treat called *gulab jamun*.

> Always ask an adult to help when cooking foods in oil.

Ingredients

SYRUP

- 100 ml water
- 200 g caster sugar
- ¼ teaspoon ground cardamom

DOUGH

- 225 g instant dry milk powder
- 110 g plain flour
- 1¼ teaspoon baking powder
- ½ teaspoon baking soda
- 125 ml whole milk
- 25 g butter (unsalted), melted
- 1 teaspoon lemon juice
- 2 tablespoons plain natural yoghurt
- 1 litre vegetable oil (for frying)

Equipment

- scales
- large saucepan with lid
- mixing bowl
- medium saucepan
- slotted spoon
- plate with paper towels

SAFETY FIRST
Ask an adult for help when using the hob.

Method

1. Mix the water, sugar and cardamom together in a saucepan over a medium. heat. Stir until the sugar dissolves. Turn down the heat and simmer for 5 minutes until it has thickened into a syrup and set it aside.

2. Mix the milk powder, flour, baking powder and baking soda together in a bowl. Add the butter, milk, lemon juice and yoghurt and mix it into a dough until it is soft and slightly sticky. Let it rest for 5 minutes.

3. Roll small pieces of the dough into small balls, about 3 cm in size. They should be smooth with no cracks.

4. Fill half a saucepan with oil. Ask an adult to heat the oil over a medium heat. Place the dough balls into the oil and cook for 2 to 3 minutes until they are brown on all sides. Ask an adult to lift the balls out with a slotted spoon.

5. Place the fried dough into the syrup and bring it back to a boil. Remove the saucepan from the heat and cover with the lid. Leave the dough to soak up the syrup for several hours.

6. Warm the *gulab jamuns* up in the syrup before serving.

TOP TIP:

If you want a bit more flavour, you can add a few drops of rosewater and a pinch of saffron to the syrup.

Noodle Kugel (Dairy noodle casserole)

Eating dairy is a Hanukkah tradition to celebrate Judith's heroic story.

Ingredients

- 155 g margarine
- 450 g medium noodles, cooked and drained
- 250 g digestive biscuits, well crumbled
- 235 g cottage cheese
- 115 g cream cheese
- 235 g sour cream
- 6 large eggs
- 300 g caster sugar
- ½ teaspoon cinnamon
- 1 can pie filling (cherry or apple)

TOP TIP:

Cook the noodles al dente (firm) as it will continue to cook in the casserole and you don't want it to turn to mush.

Equipment

- large ovenproof baking tin
- scales
- saucepan
- strainer
- electric whisk
- food processor
  (or resealable plastic bag and rolling pin)
- bowls

SAFETY FIRST

Ask an adult for help when using the hob or oven.

Method

1. Preheat the oven to 180°C or gas mark 4. Meanwhile boil the noodles in a pot for 5 to 10 minutes and drain them once done.

2. Grease a baking tin. Mix the biscuit crumbs with 100 g of melted margarine. Press the mixture onto the bottom and sides of the greased tin.

3. Mix the cottage cheese, cream cheese, sour cream and 55 g of melted margarine together.

4. Whisk the eggs for at least 10 minutes until they are very thick. Add 250 g of sugar and beat for another 5 minutes. Combine this with the cheese mixture.

5. Pour the mixture over the noodles and stir well. Spoon into the baking tin.

6. Mix 50 g of sugar with the cinnamon and sprinkle over the top of the casserole. Bake for 50 minutes, until all the liquid has been absorbed.

7. Ask an adult to insert a knife into the casserole – if it's cooked it will come out clean. Remove the casserole from the oven and cover it with the pie filling. Return it to the oven and bake for another 10 minutes.

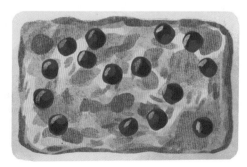

Marshmallow Dreidl

This *dreidl*-inspired treat is as much fun to make as it is to eat! You can serve them on a tray during a Hanukkah party.

Ingredients

INGREDIENTS FOR 11 DREIDLS:

- 1 360 g bar of Toblerone (cut into 11 separate triangles)
- 11 extra large marshmallows
- 11 thin pretzel sticks (for *dreidl* handles)
- 350 g dark chocolate
- 100 g white chocolate

INGREDIENTS FOR EDIBLE GLUE:

- 120 g icing sugar
- 2 tablespoons unsalted butter, softened
- ¼ teaspoon vanilla
- 1-2 teaspoons milk

Equipment

- scales
- skewer or sharp knife
- whisk
- small bowl
- tray covered in parchment paper
- microwave-safe bowl (for melting chocolate)
- large plate lined with baking parchment
- piping bag (or resealable plastic bag with the corner snipped off)

SAFETY FIRST

Ask an adult for help when using a knife.

Method

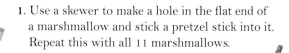

1. Use a skewer to make a hole in the flat end of a marshmallow and stick a pretzel stick into it. Repeat this with all 11 marshmallows.

2. Whisk the icing sugar, butter and vanilla together in a mixing bowl. Slowly add milk until it is sticky – if it gets too watery, add a bit of sugar. This is your "glue".

3. Dip the base of a chocolate triangle into the mixture and place a marshamallow on to it. Place on a tray lined with parchment paper and let it dry for 20 minutes until it is completely set. Repeat for all 11 marshmallows.

4. Place the dark chocolate in a microwaveable bowl and heat it until it melts. Stir it every 30 seconds so that it heats all the way through. Let it cool for 5 minutes

5. Holding onto the pretzel end, dip the marshmallow into the chocolate so both the marshmallow and the Toblerone triangle are completely covered. Repeat with all your marshmallows and place on a large plate lined with parchment paper. Leave them in the fridge to set.

6. Meanwhile, melt the white chocolate in the microwave and place it into a piping bag. Draw Hebrew letters onto each *dreidl*.

7. Put back in the fridge until fully set.

Schnitzel (Fried chicken cutlet)

Schnitzel is a favourite European food, dating back many centuries. The Jewish version is usually made of a boneless piece of chicken or turkey, dipped in an egg, breaded and then fried in oil. In Israel, it is often coated with paprika or sesame seeds for extra flavour. Feel free to experiment.

> Always ask an adult to help when cooking foods in oil.

Ingredients

- 6 boneless, skinless chicken breasts
- 50 g plain flour
- salt
- ground black pepper
- 4 large eggs, whites only
- 200 g breadcrumbs (seasoned or add a bit of thyme)
- 1 teaspoon sesame seeds or paprika (optional)
- vegetable oil (for frying)
- 1 lemon, cut into wedges (optional)

Equipment

- scales
- baking tray
- chopping board
- knife
- cling film
- mallet (or rolling pin)
- 3 bowls
- large frying pan
- plate lined with paper towels

SAFETY FIRST
Ask an adult for help when using the hob or a knife.

Method

1. Ask an adult to "butterfly" each chicken breast. Cut through the meat from the thicker side to the thinner side – don't cut all the way through. Spread the chicken out.

2. Cover each piece of chicken with cling film. Ask an adult to pound them with a mallet until they are equally thin all over.

3. Fill a bowl with flour and season it with salt and pepper. In a second bowl add 3 or 4 egg whites. Pour the breadcrumbs into another bowl and mix in the sesame seeds or paprika, if you like.

4. Pour a bit of oil into the frying pan and put it on a medium heat. Take a chicken breast and bread it by dipping it into the bowl of flour, then the egg whites and finally the breadcrumbs.

5. Ask an adult to gently place the chicken into the oil. Cook each side for 3 minutes until it is brown. Place the chicken on a plate lined with paper towels. Repeat with the remaining chicken.

6. Schnitzel is delicious when eaten immediately, especially with a bit of lemon squeezed on top of it.

TOP TIP:

Open the windows before you start frying or your kitchen will smell like oil for hours!

Gelt Hot Chocolate

Ingredients

FOR EACH MUG OF HOT CHOCOLATE:

- 230 ml milk
- 1 teaspoon cocoa powder
- 3 large chocolate coins
  (or about 15 g chocolate)

Equipment

- saucepan
- whisk
- mug for each person
- spoon

SAFETY FIRST

Remove the foil and be
careful when pouring the
hot milk onto the chocolate
coins to melt them. You
can also melt them using
a microwave.

Method

1. Ask an adult to heat the milk and cocoa powder in a small saucepan over medium heat until steaming hot. Whisk to dissolve the cocoa.

2. Remove the foil from the chocolate coins and place them into a mug.

3. Ask an adult to pour the hot chocolate milk into the mug and let it melt the chocolate coins for a few minutes.

4. Use a spoon to mix the melted chocolate coins, then enjoy immediately.

My Hanukkah

My Hanukkah ✶ Day 1

Date: _____

I spent tonight with: _____

_____

We ate: _____

My favourite part of today was:

_____

_____

_____

My Goals for the coming year

A key aspect of Judaism is about helping others and improving yourself.

On this page, record three things you want to do in the next year to help other people. This might be saving some of your pocket money regularly to give to charity. Or perhaps you're going to pick up rubbish to make the area you live in cleaner, or help your parents by doing some extra chores.

My Hanukkah Memories

Use this space to keep a record of any special Hanukkah memories.

Memories

Glossary

Apocrypha – collection of sacred books that were written after the Hebrew Bible (c.300 BCE–c.300 CE).

Ashkenazi Jew – Jews with German, French and Eastern European ancestry.

Empire – a large area of land or people that are under the rule of one person.

Gregorian calendar – the most commonly used calendar in modern times. This calendar is divided into twelve months and most years have 365 days.

Hanukkiah – on Hanukkah, Jews light a special menorah with nine branches – it has one branch for each day of the holiday, plus one extra 'helper' candle.

Hesed – Jews perform acts of hesed, where they support others in non-financial ways. These include: visiting the sick, comforting the mourner, giving the dead an honourable burial and offering hospitality to those who need it.

Kosher – Hebrew word meaning "fit", it refers to the dietary laws many Jews follow, like not eating pork or shellfish and not mixing dairy foods with meat.

Mizrahi Jew – Jews whose ancestry is from Middle Eastern countries, such as Iraq, Iran and Yemen and Morocco. Mizrahi comes from the Hebrew word *mizrah*, which means "eastern".

Monotheistic – refers to those religions, such as Judaism, Christianity and Islam, that believe in one God.

Oppressed – someone who is subjected to an unjust use of authority.

Pirsum haNes – a key ritual of Hanukkah, where Jews publicize and share the miracle of light. The hanukkiah is placed in a window so that others can see it.

Rabbi – a religious leader in Judaism. Rabbis today study Jewish texts for many years so that they are qualified to lead their community.

Reconsecrate – to make sacred and formally rededicate it to a religious purpose.

Sephardic Jew – people who are descended from Jews who moved to Spain and Portugal (and later North Africa, the Netherlands and other areas of Europe). Sephardic comes from the Hebrew word *sepharad*, meaning Spain.

Shabbat – a Hebrew word that means "to rest". It is the Jewish day of rest which runs each week from sunset on Friday to sunset on Saturday. During *Shabbat*, Jews rest from work and enjoy a day spent with family, friends and God.

Shammash – the Hebrew word for "helper". The shammash is a special candle that is used to light all of the other candles on each night of Hanukkah.

Talmud – often referred to as the Oral Torah, it is believed to have been given to Moses by God on Mount Sinai at the same time as he was given the written Torah. The Oral Torah was passed down for many generations as an oral teaching until it was written down by ancient rabbis. The Oral Torah contains the Talmud, an important document that expands on the written Torah to helps Jews incorporate its teachings into their everyday life.

Torah – it contains the Five Books of Moses, which make up the beginning of the Jewish Bible. Jews and Christians believe it was revealed to the Israelites at Mount Sinai in ancient times and contains the story of their relationship with God, as well as the moral, religious and civil laws that govern Jewish life.

Tzedakah – the Jewish obligation to give money to the poor. Even someone who receives it has to give some of that tzedakah to someone less fortunate!

Yiddish – a language historically spoken by Ashkenazi Jews.

About the Author

SHOSHANA BOYD GELFAND is a rabbi, speaker and writer whose passion is bringing Jewish wisdom into the public sphere. As such, Shoshana presents regularly on BBC Radio, teaches in multiple interfaith settings and is the author of *The Barefoot Book of Jewish Folk Tales*, a collection of Jewish stories for all faiths and all ages.

About the Illustrator

KATHRYN SELBERT is a freelance illustrator and designer currently living in Montclair, New Jersey, USA, with her French bulldog Margot and tea-loving husband. She earned her BFA in Illustration from the Rhode Island School of Design. Her work is inspired by the people she meets in her everyday life, our colourful world, flora and fauna, and having fun.